My Dad Is a GRAVEDIGGER

Story by
Andrew Markey

The story, all names, characters, and incidents portrayed in this production are fictitious. No identification with actual persons (living or deceased), places, buildings, and products is intended or should be inferred.

Copyright © 2025 by Andrew Markey.
All rights reserved.

The text in this book was selected, arranged, and organized by the author, while the images were generated with the assistance of artificial intelligence. These images serve as an immersive supplement to the story and were carefully reviewed to align with the author's vision.

First paperback printing June 2025.

ISBN 979-8-3493-6099-2 (paperback)

For my dad, Daryl

*And in loving memory of my brother,
Matthew Robert Markey
(1984-2025)*

When someone dies, they are sometimes put into the ground at a special place called a cemetery, or graveyard.

Many people are buried in cemeteries. To remember them, a gravestone with their name is placed where they are buried.

My dad is a gravedigger. He works at a cemetery and uses a big machine to dig a deep hole in the ground. This is called a grave.

My dad helps set up chairs, a tent, and other pieces of equipment at the grave before the person is buried.

The body of the dead is kept in a coffin made of wood or metal. A special car called a hearse brings the coffin to the cemetery.

At the funeral, family and friends gather around the grave to say goodbye before the coffin is carefully lowered into the ground.

The tractor can get very dirty after a burial, so my dad will wash it and check for any damage so that he can dig another grave tomorrow.

When the grass grows too long at the graveyard, my dad will cut it with a riding mower—even when it's really hot in the summer!

Bushes and trees also grow too big and they must be trimmed so that people can read the names on the gravestones.

Everyday my dad picks up trash that the wind has blown into the graveyard. A cemetery must look nice and clean at all times!

Many people visit cemeteries in the cold winter too, so my dad removes all the snow from the pathways with a plow truck.

A graveyard is not a scary place. It is a place of peace and quiet for remembering those you love and miss.

Glossary

Cemetery: a place where dead people are buried.

Coffin: a box for holding a dead person.

Funeral: a ceremony for someone who has died.

Grave: a place in the ground where a dead person is buried.

Gravedigger: a cemetery worker who digs graves.

Gravestone: a stone with writing on it that marks where a dead person is buried.

Hearse: a special car used to carry a coffin.

A treasured drawing from Andrew's grandniece

Andrew is an award-winning children's author from Michigan and comes from a family tradition of gravediggers, following the paths laid by his father and grandfather. Andrew enjoys thrilling adventures, like hot air ballooning, cruising, and mountain hiking. Yet, the highlight of his life are the memories made in South Carolina with his beloved grandniece—his ride or die.

More titles from the author

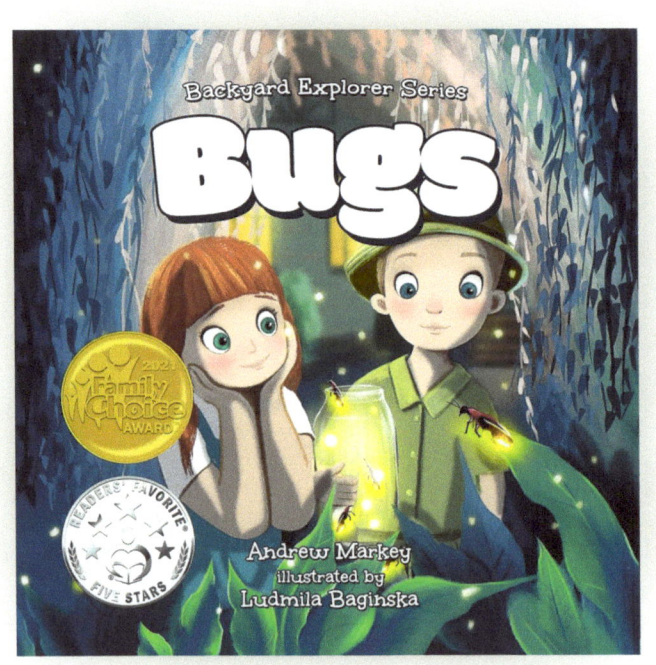

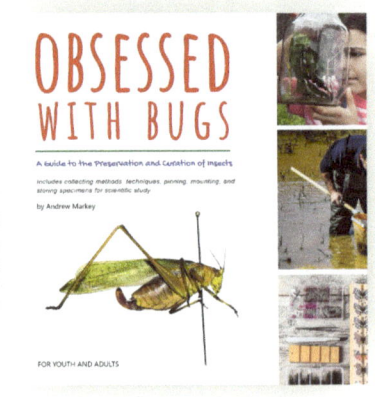

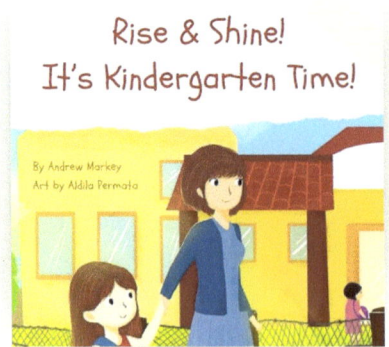

Buy online at

Amazon

Target

Barnes & Noble

Books-A-Million

Walmart

www.ingramcontent.com/pod-product-compliance
Lightning Source LLC
LaVergne TN
LVHW071700060526
838201LV00037B/391